THE DETROITIST

AN ANTHOLOGY ABOUT DETROIT

MARSHA MUSIC

Copyright © 2019 by Marsha Battle Philpot, "Marsha Music"

All rights reserved.

Edited and Published by Detroit Ink Publishing, Detroit Michigan
www.detroitinkpublishing.com

Front Cover Photograph © 2019 Jeff Cancelosi

Back Cover Photograph © 2019 Brad Ziegler

"Kidnapped Children of Detroit" Graphic © Kathy Rashid

Cover Designed and Book Printed by Valley Publishing Company, a division of Mays Multimedia Southfield, Michigan www.maysmedia.us

Published and Printed in the USA

No part of this book may be reproduced in any form or by any electronic or mechanical means, including information storage and retrieval systems, without written permission from the author, except for the use of brief quotations in a book review.

CONTENTS

1. Memories and Dreams   1
2. The Kidnapped Children of Detroit   7
3. Just Say Hi! (The Gentrification Blues)   21
4. A Poem for Belle Isle   33
5. Jolene   51

    About the Author   61

1
MEMORIES AND DREAMS

From the mire and murky loam,

Bottom Black with Dusky soil

The First People walked this land

Heard the river's rush and roar

Near the water Savoyard

there in battles took a stand

made the fateful crimson flow
near the strait called Le D'etroit
From Black Bottom's swamp and fog
Green and verdant ribbons grew
lush farms risen from the bog
furs and stoves and ironworks

∼

From the briny underground
there arose a great world noise
symphony of city sounds
sights and wonders to behold
Hear inventions' hum and clang
foundry's fire and factory's bang,
listen to assembly lines,
hear production's sturm und drang

Hear the hiss of molten iron
turning into Model A's
listen to the shouts of hires
working for five dollar days.

Nations gathered in this place
varied hues and diverse face

working people prospering

but segregate the darker race

clack and clatter of streetcars

sounds of great Grand Central trains

immigrants and great migrations

streets are *packed* between shift change

Come from Europe, up from South

workers moving all about

roads and streets exhaling steam!

hiss and whining of machines

Autos rolling off the line

make the rhythm of the time

Hark! the notes of human toiling

hear the shouts of labor's roiling

Moneymakers pulling strings

busting blocks, dividing streets

profits made by real estate

instigating fright and hate

driven out by greed and guile

leaving city streets behind

Sounds of flight across 8 mile

did naught to stop the city's sound

Blues and Jazz and Gospel flowed

and record shops were all around

but came the news from City Hall

Black Bottom is to be destroyed

And then to make a new freeway

Hastings Street gets wrecking-balled

Black Bottom gone, and Hastings dead

So many to the Westside fled

But drum rolls for equality

all went unheard, no scrutiny

and so the rage and fire burned

in '67s mutiny

Generations now have gone

destruction changed the city's song

But now their children do return

From exile, coming back to learn

With sounds of electronica

and Techno beats made in this town

I open arms to welcome them

The ones who really want to live

amidst we folks who never left

Reside together with respect

Some say they come to save Detroit

But *I* say, they come to BE saved.

2

THE KIDNAPPED CHILDREN OF DETROIT

It happened suddenly.

One day, we'd be outside with our friends, black, brown, and white, on the warm summer days before the start of the next school semester, playing jacks and hopscotch, riding bikes.

The next day, our white friends would be gone. One of my friends might have said, "Hey, we're moving," in the middle of a game of kickball, but there were few real goodbyes, or promises to keep in touch, at least not of the type associated with the farewells of kids who had been together all or most of their lives.

In the jumbled mishmash of childhood memories during those

transitional years, I recall worshippers leaving the neighborhood church after Sunday service, descending the dark oak staircase from the sanctuary.

In their hurry to get on with their day, it looked, from my kid-level gaze, like a stampede, during those late summer days when our integrated neighborhood was disassembling before my eyes.

I will forever associate the Sunday-dressed hemlines and dark-suited pants legs with their rushing, running to get away—from us—the worshippers with whom they had just fellowshipped before God.

White parents were grabbing their kids and escaping from Detroit—and from its enclave Highland Park, where I grew up, a then solidly middle-class enclave within Detroit's borders, "a city within a city." Often, it appeared as if they left in the dark of the night, the moves seemed so clandestine.

This sense of them leaving virtually "overnight," packing up and disappearing, was likely due to the white parents' reluctance to speak to their black neighbors—whom they often treated with pronounced neighborliness—about their impending moves, knowing that their departures were largely because of the color of the neighbors' skin.

I wonder if some worried that their daytime public neighborliness contrasted with their nighttime kitchen table planning, their plotting to get out of the neighborhood as soon as they could manage. Perhaps they forbade their children to speak to their darker friends about the frenetic packing going on inside.

Certainly they didn't want to speak of the reason for the moves with the reason for the moves—though everyone, of course, knew why. Or they talked to their black neighbors pretending "those new people moving in" didn't include those with whom they commiserated. But one by one, the white families left their old homes, tree-lined streets—and us—behind.

I'm sure that some of my friends listened to their parents in their homes, as they spoke of us with words of racial hatred, while outside they smiled across backyard fences, making small talk about sod and azaleas. Perhaps black and white neighbors rarely communicated at all during this time, when our neighborhoods were soon to be re-segregated. For there was virulent racism and ill-disguised violence in areas throughout the city, and even in the late '60s, blacks could not shop in many stores.

Detroit was replete with episodes of unrest and even terror in the competition over housing: whites demanded that blacks be stopped from moving into an east side housing project, which precipitated a race riot in 1943.

A generation before that, Ossian Sweet, a black medical doctor, was met with mobs as he moved into his home in a white neighborhood on the near east side. Clarence Darrow would defend Sweet's right to defend his hearth, and establish, "A man's home is his castle."

My grandmother told me the tale of how, in the early '50's, she had saved up the money she made as a domestic to buy a home on Clairmont and Woodward Avenue. On the eve of the closing, the realtor came to her with the news that the white block club did not want her in the neighborhood.

Grandmother refused to change her plans and sent him packing, but the realtor returned—the block club offered to pay her back the money for her down payment, plus some. Well, Grandmother took the money and ran, to a neighborhood on the near east side.

She moved near Conant Gardens, a community developed on land that had been owned by an abolitionist named Shubael Conant, who refused to sell his land to developers who sold homes with the restrictive covenants that were common in Detroit.

That community was one of the first strongholds of black middle class home ownership. My grandmother chuckled at the end of her story, at the irony that by the time of her telling, thirty years later, Clairmont and Woodward was all black—the block club had obviously been unable to buy its way against the changing times.

Some whites, I'm sure, were not influenced by race baiting, but left the city solely to experience the new suburban living, or to be closer to the jobs that had moved across 8 Mile—though they knew that they were going to communities where blacks were not allowed.

Some of my friends' parents were surely anguished about the decision to move, sometimes leaving behind equity and often their own parents who refused to go. Did my young white friends listen to their planning with conflicted feelings? Never mind; the torrent of change and fear that was driving white Detroiters could not be turned off.

And so, I say, my friends were kidnapped; snatched away from their homes, often under cover of night or in rushed moves that split friends apart for a lifetime. I watched Mary Martin fly as Peter Pan on TV, and it seemed my friends too had been lured to a Neverland.

Did they cry when they were taken, missing their old friends? Did they think of what they'd left behind when they woke in homes with no deep porches or rich oaken banisters? On streets with no lush, ancient trees? Where it took a car—or two—to get anywhere, with lawns so new that grass had yet to grow?

But my friends settled into their new neighborhoods, like children do, adapting and making friends, happy for the new. Glad to be in the modern houses on spread-out blocks, out of the brick behemoths, two-family flats, or frame houses of the old, dense Detroit streets they'd left behind.

One of my friends remembers the overwhelming fear that consumed his family's 7 Mile and Wyoming household—a relatively new community even then—as they prepared to leave for Southfield. He confirms that, in so many homes, there was a sense of panic, as his family prepared not just to move, but to escape, as if from some impending debacle.

He recalls how, in the innocence of youth, he wondered about the reason for the terror; for it appeared to him that the black folks moving into his neighborhood were at the very least, in his child's eye view of social classes, the most non-scary folks in the world: doctors, teachers, professionals. To him, they seemed to be of a clearly higher social standing than most of the folks who were desperately moving out.

It happened rapidly. An elder of my church remembers that he started school in his west-side neighborhood as only one of two black children in his kindergarten class; the rest were white, mostly Jewish. By the time he left elementary school, only two white children remained.

The Jewish exodus (so to speak) was an integral engine of the movement of blacks across the west side, for they were willing to break the "restrictive covenants" in deeds that had prohibited homeowners from selling to blacks, and often Jews too. Block by block, as whites moved out, Jewish homeowners replaced them and then blacks followed, with synagogues transformed into black churches.

After the 1967 riots (also known as "The Rebellion," in which my own father's record business was destroyed), the post-conflagration trauma was so great, and the consciousness of Detroiters so altered by the eruption of turmoil and destruction, that it came to be said that "all the white people left after '67," a false narrative that persists even today.

In reality, the exit from the city began after World War II. By 1952, the construction of Northland Mall in suburban Southfield had begun, to accommodate the mounting loss of population from Detroit; it became the first and largest suburban mall in the country.

Whites bought new houses in the newly built suburbs, when the schools in the city were still quite good; and really, there was no reason to go except for a change of scenery and a good use of the G.I. Bill.

But blacks were straining against the "James Crow" segregation of the North, and out of the packed neighborhoods in which they had been confined. Millions of whites were worked into moving van frenzy by word-of-mouth from one home to the other, and in rabble-rousing community meetings.

Importantly, real estate interests and developers—often individually, and surely cumulatively, stood to profit greatly in that rapid turnover of properties.

Some real estate companies grew rich from this race-based trading in hope and fear. Some actually identified neighborhoods and instigated the whole cycle in order to profit from the terror-driven turnover of properties.

One of my friends remembers when her white neighborhood was inundated with flyers, exhorting Whites to get away from the coming dark hordes.

Neighborhoods had brief, uneasy periods of "integration," marked by racial tension and police brutality, before the last of the whites would move out.

This practice is called "block-busting," creating a crazy, predictable cycle—whites move out, lured by real estate interests to leave for white communities; blacks move in and fear is escalated; whites become panicked and, egged on by the realtors and block associations, sell at ever lower prices in order to hurry and "get out."

This also happened when blacks moved into communities paying higher rents or land-contract prices than the whites before them. The more whites that moved out, "dumping" houses onto the market, the more blacks were able to move in; many of them were on a lower economic rung than those who preceded them, creating a self-fulfilling prophecy.

The result—a neighborhood that had solidly "middle class" or even affluent blacks and whites, had, in a few short years, a preponderance of poorer families. These were families who were often less able to maintain the lifestyle in that neighborhood, and brought with them the problems that their children often had in rough projects or poorer communities.

Many of my black friends from harsher backgrounds had a difficult time adjusting to the quiet, tree-lined life on their new blocks. In each neighborhood, they used the drugs that were flooding into the communities to deal with their anxieties of being planted in these short-lived "mixed" communities, where they were often not wanted by blacks *or* whites. This accelerated the neighborhood's crime and disruption—the final death-knell for many communities.

Another factor I remember that prompted moves to the suburbs was violence, whether threatened or carried out, against white kids, who were often tormented by black kids in outbursts of retaliation for wrongs real or imagined.

Later, there was the bussing of children to schools as a tactic to address the re-segregation of the community, with the rise of agitators who whipped up a frenzy of racial fear and hatred, driving whites further across 8 Mile.

A group of us stared down Klan sympathizers on the east side, singing "We Shall Overcome" in the streets during chilling episodes of anti-bussing turmoil.

As people left, so did businesses; the suburbs, an appealing, all-white commercial for modern living, were a vacuum sucking life and enterprise across 8 Mile. Many of the largest industrial enterprises had gone first, finding in the undeveloped suburbs the acres of land needed for the modern, stretched-out production facilities that could not be built in the property-dense city.

Companies left behind the tight neighborhoods where residents could and did join organizing efforts of all kinds, and by the 1960s, there was a freeway system to move out workers and supplies. Detroit's infrastructure, dependent upon on the former booming tax base and not the new, shrinking one, was less able to maintain services.

With joblessness that became epidemic, and the ruination of great sections of the social fabric via the scourge of crime and drugs, the urban community spiraled ever downward.

This circular, self-fulfilling, nasty game of musical chairs perpetuated itself in the Detroit area, as in other "changing" communities nationwide. As whites departed en masse, the problems they most feared came to pass. In many areas, blacks moved into a level of community that they were suddenly allowed to afford, yet unable, in the long run, to maintain.

Or, blacks with means moved into communities with aged housing stock, making the next years of living a fait accompli of devastation. Later, the 2008 mortgage crisis sealed the deal of destruction in many neighborhoods.

Even so, after white flight, there were still many communities full of dedicated residents who were paragons of home ownership, with houses and lawns maintained in consummate displays of steadfast residential pride, despite the challenges of living in the midst of flight and escalating blight.

Detroit still has exquisite blocks in affluent neighborhoods, and handsome, solid homes on working-class blocks—maintained by those who remained.

My own neighborhood, Lafayette Park, was built in 1960 to staunch the flow of white Detroiters outward. It is still a model of diverse urban living, with those who live there committed to the city.

During the departures in the late '60s, my next-door neighbors were among the last whites to leave our block; we had lived next door to them all of our lives. He was president of a bank on Woodward Avenue, and on the verge of retirement, but I guess the changing times had become too much; whites were now moving at the sound of the drum beat of the Black Power era.

The banker's wife, a white-haired lady who had known me since I was a babe, literally burst into tears across the backyard fence at the sight of my brand new sixties Afro, and asked me tearfully why I had to wear my hair "like that." Shortly after, it was time for them to go.

Some waited too long and moved into white communities in which they were branded by the stigma of having come from neighborhoods that had long ago turned black, never to be viewed as really equal to the whites in their new towns.

But they were all transfigured into new souls called suburbanites, though many maintained an undying love-hate relationship with the neighborhoods they were forced by fear to leave behind, often viewing the city and its current residents with a mixture of contempt, dismay, and nostalgia.

They pined for the old glory days of the city, following the stories of its streets and politics as if they lived within its boundaries; following the news of its decline like a lover both grieving and gloating over the travails of a lost love.

In the late sixties, many of my black friends began to leave too, as the city declined, for segregation had finally lifted its weight from the close-lying suburbs. So they too moved across 8 Mile.

Over the years I've known many whites who work in downtown Detroit, and savor the scary, sexy power of being comfortable in the city—at least during work hours.

They're proud of their ability to move around the urban landscape and to have at least daytime friends of other colors. Most whites in the Detroit area stay away, especially from anywhere outside of downtown, fearful of the community.

But some former Detroiters are pulled back to their old neighborhoods—some intact, some bedraggled, some where the old home is completely gone: the decay and destruction an affirmation of their parents' obviously right decision to leave, so long ago.

I wonder if, sometimes, they suspect that somehow, that decision itself, multiplied across Detroit, was at least part of the cause of all the mess here now. That maybe the mass flight, the leaving of property all over town, the years of being egged on by whispers and realtors to cross 8 Mile, was all part of a nasty, self-destructive Monopoly game—with real properties and real lives.

I also wonder what might have happened in Detroit if there had never been this flight—if whites had held on and resisted the racial manipulation, if blacks had been able to push back the plague of unemployment, drugs and crime, if we had been able to live in Detroit, all at one time.

It is hard for many black Detroiters to comprehend the sense of belonging, or even entitlement, that many whites feel toward Detroit, even decades and states removed from living within city boundaries. There are those—black and white—who have never lived in Detroit proper, or even in Michigan, who gaze (through Google Maps) at old family homesteads, and vicariously traverse old family blocks from afar.

They regard Detroit as *their* city. And I believe that the sense of being part of Detroit proper—despite living well outside of its borders for generations—is rooted in that mass evacuation. Like the movement of blacks across the city after the destruction of Black Bottom, this was an unprecedented transfer of community; and suburban parents did their best, as they understood it, to build better lives. But fear of a black city made my friends Detroiters in Exile.

Folks ask the question, Will Detroit come back? Well, Detroit never left—but three generations did. Today, regardless of the city's efforts at redevelopment, most know that they will never again live in the city of their affection.

Most of the old neighborhoods are much too far from livability for them, and the city's core and urban lifestyle holds no appeal for those accustomed to suburban sprawl. But more and more of the children and grandchildren of the Kidnapped Children are finding their way home.

But despite ghost-town metaphors, blank-slate pronouncements, and prairie-land descriptions of Detroit, they find the city already occupied, and these strangers in a strange yet familiar land must learn to share it with those who held on.

As the quality of life in the outer ring of the city declined, forcing more blacks to look outward to escape crime and to seek neighborhood stability, property values fell in the near suburbs—because of the age of those cities and their housing stock, because of the mortgage crisis, because of blockbusting that is still alive and well (though sometimes with more subtle practices than before).

As many of the suburbs become less "exclusive" and downtown living grows, owners who held onto core city properties during the crash of their values watch their fortunes rise, after contributing to the city's vistas of decay and destruction.

For decades, they held onto ravaged, abandoned structures as they waited for a time of profitability, contributing to much of the urban devastation for which black city dwellers have been reviled.

Younger generations of whites from the suburbs, who don't have their forebears' fear of the city, are moving in the opposite direction, proudly proclaiming their Detroit provenance and reveling in their new urban life. Some of them recreate suburban segregation in the heart of the city; they want life in Detroit—without Detroiters.

But many more look to the city as the most exciting place in the world to live in diversity. They are led by the artists' community, the creative seraphim of redevelopment; they are the coal-mine canaries of our scorched and burned land. This community of artists has been waiting and creating for such a time as this, for Detroit has always been a city of artists.

Our extreme maker impulse in Detroit is now unfettered, no longer consumed by the past that propelled, yet devoured, so much of the city's creative energy. They are side-by-side with those who've held on for decades, trying to make "a way out of no way."

As in South Africa, there is a need for atonement in Detroit and its suburbs. We need a restorative movement to heal what has happened here, as the working people of this town ,competed against themselves over the right to the good life. We have to share stories about the experiences of the past era.

As we move forward in Detroit, there must be a mending of the human fabric that was rent into municipal pieces with the divisions of city and suburbs. Small, continual acts of reconciliation are called for here, as sections of the city rise again.

As the children and grandchildren of the Kidnapped Children make their way to the city, I believe that it is the responsibility of the rest of us—those who, like me, never left—to welcome them; to tell our new residents the real city narratives, to share the truths of what happened here from all sides.

There are deep schisms that never should have been, that were orchestrated by self-serving interests; we must work to mend these wherever possible. Our new residents have a contagious earnestness, energy, and hopefulness, reminiscent of the movements of our past, and there's a difference between their sincere efforts for change and the machinations of those who would manipulate the urban crisis to their own benefit, casting us aside like flotsam in the name of progress.

Yet it is likewise the charge of our new Detroiters to acknowledge and respect those already here—to actually SEE longtime residents, for we are not invisible. Our new residents must learn from our history and experience; they must work alongside our earlier residents and their children in Detroit's renewal, for they are the bedrock of the redeveloped city and the nexus of its future.

Let us figure out—this time—how to live together, so that more children and grandchildren of the Kidnapped Children can come home to live in the city, so that more of our children and grandchildren might also be part of a truly new Detroit. Young people come to be freed from their lives of suburban isolation and the crippling divisions of this region; they want to be a part of a new urban reality.

It is true that some say that they have come to save Detroit, but I say, they come to Detroit to BE saved.
With special thanks to editor Anna Clark
who originally published the Kidnapped Children of Detroit

3

JUST SAY HI! (THE GENTRIFICATION BLUES)

Originally published in the Detroit cultural journal, Infinite Mile; and in London's Hero Magazine, below:

All around Detroit we talk,

from shops to congregations

There's much discussion of the city's new Gentrification

and all the changes with the folks a'moving to the D

the changes in our lifetime thought we'd never live to see

We talk about The Newcomers, with righteous consternation,

ol' school exasperation, 'bout a disconcerting thing –

"They don't even SPEAK!" we say, when we get on the subject

our mantra of rejection of in-vi-si-bi-lity

Our indignation hides the sting of truly being unseen,

of being looked – right through – in our own city

Ralph Ellison, he wrote of this so many years ago

Walk past and never turn an eye to see us oh! what pity!

Detroit's a place wherein we "speak" to you in varied tones

Hey! Hi! Hello! How ya' doin'? Whazzup? What's happ'nen'? Whaddup Doe!

Detroit is widely said to be a big, small southern town

the separation's one or two degrees, is what we've found

We nod our heads at passersby; acknowledge other folks

Goes back to railroads underground, rebukes of ol' Jim Crow

We do affirm and say a word to those whom we pass by

A simple thing but means a lot to us, so

Just Say Hi!

From Ottawa, the Huron and the Potawatomi

Then French and Europeans, enslaved Blacks came to be free

an immigration influx, then a torrent from the South

The People Of Detroit, 'tis true they come from many routes

To old Black Bottom's death, and then the birth of Lafayette Park

Old strip farms, townships, properties, transitions we've embarked

Horses, autos; racetracks, roads; now Slow Roll rules the lanes

The time has come, it has begun, Detroit sees change, again

Newcomers here will walk with us into the coming years,

Join those of us who've still held on, see how we've persevered

We faced upheavals through the years, that caused Detroiters many tears

So now, again we rearrange – the lifeblood of this town is Change

Just Say Hi!

Black Folks (Whites, too) whom I've long known, who've lived here for a lifetime,

discuss Newcomers frequently – Midtown, Downtown and 'round town –

who move to 'hoods as more each day they're priced out of the core

but bring excited spirits to the corners of Detroit

We have to tell the difference from among those who are new

The ones sincere and earnest and respect both me and you

For most of those who're coming here, they love this city, too

But we all know there're those who just have dollars in their view

Just Say Hi!

Now some deny they gentrify in devastated D,

they move to empty spaces – no displacement they can see

and think that since the building stock was emptied long ago,

no one's displaced from this old place, so no one's had to go

But don't forget our memories are carved deep into our souls

We lived, and worked, took care of biz, then time for us to roll

They pushed us, moved us, crime'd us out, then time did take its toll

those barren places all stood guard; we drove by, walked past old facades,

then decades hence, we were replaced – just took long years to fill the space,

It matters not how long it takes; oh yes, we've still been gentrified.

And here's a new twist to the game – those Newcomers that were so brave

or smart or poor or hopeful, strong; or techno, hip or all strung out

or artful, slick or really savvy – arrived before big money landed

they get eviction noticed too – and pushed from Downtown by the new

Now they share in other's fate and seek new rents at lower rates – gentri*fried*

Just Say Hi!

But yes, there's gentrifying norm, folks old and frail with bodies worn

or recovering from drink or drugs; grateful, proud of old, quiet rooms,

in big apartments in Downtown, on "ghost town" streets, they lived in peace,

grateful in their sober lives, a place to rest from dark to dawn

or kids who made the DJ sounds, the techno parties, drew the crowds

Downtown when it wasn't cool, kept the buildings from emptying out

Landlords got their Section 8, win-win in Downtown Detroit's Dark days

Now realtors come to speculate, announce that they will renovate

Open back at "market rates" – time to shop for another place

Just Say Hi!

We talk about the buildings, all the barren, ragged mastodons,

old factories, shops and corner stores, warehouse structures, built to last

Ghoulish hulks of prosperity past, when streets weren't split by overpass

Ghastly end-days totems rise, burn retinal scars in children's' eyes

owned by investor absentees, awaiting days when values rise

vultures trying just to see, the profit possibilities

We co-exist with nightmares-scapes, the charred and grisly devastated

built environs (and 'fore our eyes, the Heidelberg becomes a pyre)

The ruin porn photographers are clever choreographers

of images that skew the way, we live here in Detroit each day

Worship ruins like religion, treat our protest with derision

they love that urban detritus, with little care of what hurts us

Just Say Hi!

You see, we live on many blocks that seem unaltered by the clock

With neighborhoods of much good care, of lovely lawns and kept-up yards

and look, with just a camera's twist, it seems as if we don't exist

But now Newcomers have arrived, our neighborhoods get newly eyed

and even so, for sure we know, how hard we fought to keep our homes

and though we know we were ignored, our labor was its own reward

for our beloved city rests, on many shoulders that were blessed

We had no time to feel bereft, we carried on when others left

Just Say Hi!

We speak of the Abandonment, of the great leaving years ago

Plants and stores and factories, taking jobs and money flow

We arrived, the neighbors left, not so much fled, but *driven* out

across 8 Mile, pawns in a game, of money makers, turning land

and properties, over again and again

Run out, I'd say by their own fear, manipulated by the hands

that instigated; profiteers, that made the money as they ran

and as they left their busted-blocks, and fled their grand homes lock and stock.

I wonder what it did it to us, to watch them flee and scorn us thus

Just Say Hi!

We talk about foreclosures, of the forcing out and moving in

the transfers of this property impacts all generations kin

We speak of landlords who deny, a yearly lease in many shops

and make their tenants month-to-month, a'waiting for their big jackpot

We talk about the magic way that blocks and lots and streets turn safe

as with the turning of a switch, or raising of some unseen flag

on top of newly conquered land, where seems they take some unseen stand

They jog and walk and skate with ease, in places we don't dare drive streets

We talk of all new words for things – old 'hoods are now called villages,

there's city kids – not urban teens; beer gardens now – not liquor stores

and serve craft beers, and gourmet wines and yes, they artisanally dine

The nomenclature of the new, yet wonder if they'll speak to you

Just say Hi!

We talk around but don't admit our secret joy at seeing them,

come scout about our neighborhood or moving in, oh this is good!

or OMG – what's that we spied? A baby stroller rolling by!

For knowing that as soon they come, that with their move the trash will run

and lights turn on and cops will ride, it's back to being civilized

ignoring all our efforts past, when we grew weary with the test

and now we're old and holding on, they act as if *we* caused the mess

and knowing yet with all our years, of taxes, cutting grass, repairs

and bills and block clubs, fences fixed; we tried to rest but then transfixed

with years on hold while devil crack, made mockery of all of that

We watched the blocks of many friends be commandeered by crack house men

Now that we've had some years of peace, they've switched the drugs for bacchanals

in neighborhoods that we now share, but treated like we are not there.

by those who come here to "reclaim", as if they've just come here to gain

Just Say Hi!

Now there are those who just reject, the businesses folks who've been on deck

through all those years it wasn't cool, to shop with our entrepreneurs

Now they so often get ignored – I'm sure that sometimes they are floored –

by how Newcomers get such play, compared to those who've paved the way

But yes, I am a celebrant of signs of new development

And yes it's true, that I'm in love with more new shops and shiny stores

and watches too, and lovely styles in newfound shops and peacock aisles

I just make sure I don't forget, the ones who first did pay the debt

Just Say Hi!

We talk of The Newcomers, all their art and youthful energy

Rebuild the Third World city! They've come to save the day, you see

Like Peace Corp kids, sincere and smart, they've come to BE saved, I retort

They fall in love with urban heart, inside the city's horseshoe arc

We talk about the New Downtown, the phalanxes of suits and art

The laptops, khakis, polo tops; jobs open up like Belle Isle flowers

So many have a real head-start, inherit square feet in the city's heart

Connections and money already a part, of their success before they start

Don't get me wrong, we're happy now, at all the progress, all around,

but bitter sweetness for our own, our sons and daughters leaving home;

still taking flight so far from town, they look for work a ways around

It matters not what media says, the renaissance seems not for them

Just Say Hi!

We grieve for kids with De-troit lives so ill-prepared to step inside

the bubble of the phoenix rise, but yet we try to empathize

Newcomers step into the place, that our young folks were born to take

until their schools put on the brakes, with opportunities erased

So we must do all that we can, to reach to those who raise a hand

To pull them into new Detroit, so that they'll have great new exploits

See some Newcomers never lived, or worked around Black people here

Now find themselves creating 'burbs, right inside Detroit streets and curbs

In enclaves made for just themselves, with coffee bars and foodie shelves

They do forget that *we're* the source, of Detroit's urban cool and soul

and just remember we must share, in all of this new Detroit flair

From businesses to urban farms, we're leaders – as we always are

Just Say Hi!

Some take no time to navigate, complexities of diverse race

We're urban background, just a haze; dark corridors through which they race,

to get to the Newcomer space where they can revel in the place

of cloistered corners of the D and never try to see our face

Some come from Lions, Tigers dens and even if they lose or win

they never see us as they pass, before and aft the sport and games

There *are* Newcomers who engage, with *all* Detroiters of all age

I have a dear assemblage of, Newcomer young folks whom I love

They've rolled up sleeves and lent their skills, to push this city past its ills

Enriching lives (as they do mine), I'm grateful that I've stayed alive

To see the rebirth come along, as long as we don't push aside

the eighty plus percent of us, who've lived and worked here all the time

Some new kids who'd be a part, of everything that's 8 miles south

Can't figure how to get up close, some walk past us, just saying naught

Some come and ask me what to say, a ten-point plan? a 12-step way?

To start to the talk the Dee-troit way – it's simple:

Just say Hi!

Hi says you're in the city, and you're glad to be here with me

Hi says you share this street, this store, this wait in line, stand with me

Hi says that you don't fear we'll ask, for dollars or a quarter

Hi says you're not ignoring me, that we are *all* Detroiters

Hi says you don't mean to offend, or make the wrong reply

Hi says you just don't know what else to say, but Hi is fine

Hi says, I See You – You see Me; we're in the D together

Hi says we'll show each other how to live – we have the choice

Help me embrace you, teach you, know you – welcome to Detroit!

JUST SAY HI!

Copyright 2015 – Marsha Music

4

A POEM FOR BELLE ISLE

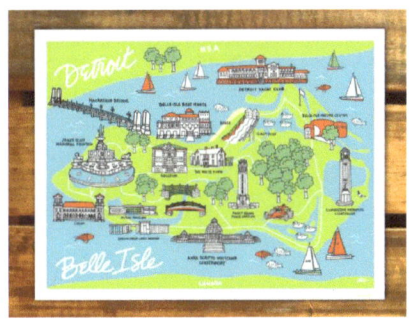

© Susi Cruz

I was asked by the Belle Isle Conservancy to write and present a poem about Belle Isle for the August 31, 2016 gathering of SOUP, a fantastic organization that raises money for new projects in Detroit. This is what I wrote, with a few revisions since.

[The sentiments expressed here are not necessarily the views of the Belle Isle Conservancy or SOUP – but they sure are mine].

• • •

When I was young and my heart cried

I went to elder woman's side

to tell her that I faced divorce

Ms. Millie told me, on her porch

"Go cry your eyes out on Belle Isle

The place we go to stay a while

to walk around and feel our grief

Among the rocks and river, weep"

She talked to me, as to a daughter

"Put your feet in Belle Isle's water

wash away the hurt and fears

go out there and cry your tears"

Her remedy I came to know

was not just hers, but many sowed

that seed, from generations' woes

just dip enough to wet the toes

The balm she often, so prescribed

was the not last time I would try

to cure my wounds or face my trials

to go and heal upon Belle Isle

But I am not the only one

to come to bask in Belle Isle sun

to walk upon the rocky shore

those days when you can take no more

In times of ache or loss of job

or episodes when life does rob

or cryin' 'bout a new heartthrob

Belle Isle is where we come to sob

The history of the Isle describes

The Ottawas, Ojibwa tribes

A-hish-in-aa-beg people dwelled

Upon the land – 'til they were felled

T'was later called the Isle of Hogs

They kept coyotes off the bog

then French and British fought to own

The island, for their kingdom's throne

Those far off countries did exploit

But finally it was Detroit's

Then Olmstead sketched it, day til dark

designed it much like Central Park

Our Belle Isle is a special place

for many folks of diverse race

But I must say, lest we forget

my people's prayers have paid the debt

Back in the old Black Bottom day

they baptized in the olden way

All draped in white they walked on down

into the river, where they found

their newborn lives, washed free of sin

emerged upon the island's rim

Down in the strait on Belle Isle's coast

was where they caught that Holy Ghost

For years Belle Isle was thusly blessed

with Saints of God in all white dress

the Spirits, in the park did rest

and kept eyes out, for those distressed

and burdened by their lives' duress
of racial ire and prejudice
Belle Isle was respite from the hate
oasis there upon the strait

But segregation on main land
moved to the island's docks and sands
the yacht and boat clubs kept us out
engineered by those with clout

Yes, through the years the city's trials
They made their way on to Belle Isle
Where Blacks and Whites enjoyed the breeze
But yet, they tarried with unease

On mainland there were poor conditions
violent racial competitions
Housing projects in demand
where soon we found that we were banned

We moved into Sojourner Truth
were met with bats and words uncouth
the Whites refused us to reside
they wouldn't let us go inside

. . .

The city heaved with animus
oh no –'twas not magnanimous
and skirmishes and hatred fanned,
the conflicts smoldering in the land

Months later, on the Belle Isle span
they broke out fighting, man to man
With racial rumors simmering
there on the Bridge in '43

Someone cried out! There was a babe
thrown from The Bridge! or was it rape?!
the gossip-mongers spread this news
both White and Black fell for the ruse

They crossed MacArthur to the streets,
men who belonged behind white sheets
They made their way to Hastings Street
their hate exploded in the heat

Inflamed Detroiters, Black and White
Erupted into racial fights
They beat us 'til so many bled

that Woodward Avenue ran red

When it was done, were many dead
the number's thirty-four, I've read
I'm making sure here, that it's said
lest we forget those days of dread

Then 'twas the time in hot July
that flames went up in Detroit skies
one fiery week in '67
the island turned its face from heaven

7,000 apprehended
overflowed Dehoco's cells
then with civil rights suspended
Belle Isle park was made a jail

Drove them in there by the busload
locked 'em up near Picnic Way
turned the buses into jail cells
where they stayed day after day

Given water, piece of bread
locked upon the buses spread-

eagled, shackled, hardly fed

some even wished that they were dead

But then old Spirits came alive

and sent an angel, to arrive

when news got out Belle Isle was jail

Judge Crockett Sr. ordered bail

But sure, we all do recollect

the better times; we resurrect

our many Belle Isle reveries

those sweet collective memories

We'd all pile up in Daddy's car

to try to find a place not far

we couldn't go up North you see

not Detroit folks who looked like me

So summer days, was time to run

out to Belle Isle for summer fun

The Boulevard to Jefferson

our route to get to Belle Isle sun

. . .

Up to McArthur Bridge we drove
and on its banks, the Giant Stove!
a testament to our old town
in days when iron-works were found

from then we'd get up to the ridge
and tunnel under, to The Bridge
while driving through, in night or morn
we'd scream! as Daddy blew the horn!

And just before we'd bbq
and grown folks started drinking brew
they'd sit on down to have a bite
and Daddy'd stop to fly a kite

We loved the big aquarium
and flower -filled solarium
and picnics, parties, that will last
in memoirs of our childhood's past

It isn't hard to reminisce
on all our dates or even trysts
We all remember that sweet kiss
while riding 'round the park in bliss

. . .

Or way back on the Lighthouse end

A quiet moment, with a friend

or even art that's there to see

the Dossin's stain-glassed masterpiece

Or weddings in the Flower House

where those betrothed became a spouse

Or family reunion days

to celebrate our DNAs

Or pony rides in olden days

with horses that we rode for pay

Or maybe we were in canoes

Traverse the inland lakes, lagoons

We rode the Slide when it was new

And took our kids to see the Zoo

Watched athletes bounding over hurtles

went to see — the Giant Turtle!

Remember winters, when we'd skate?

Upon the ice and then we'd wait

for summer; we'd shake off fatigue

play after work in baseball leagues

Some played handball on the courts
Belle Isle has had so many sports
the island was our special port
for we weren't welcome way Up North

For during summers, long and hot
Belle isle's the only place we've got
especially those who cannot pay
for leisure places, far away

But years, no budget funds to spend
It wasn't hard to comprehend
why Belle Isle suffered lack of care
and many stopped their visits there

the island looked the worse for wear
forlorn, tall grass was everywhere
few lavatories, too much trash
folks thought it cool to Belle Isle bash

But it's not true what haters said

that Belle Isle had been left for dead

It always was a wondrous place

For we who never left her grace

Decisions made to sign a lease

for thirty years, to keep the peace

upon the land and on the Isle

the State and City reconciled

The deal was done to let the State

takeover – but right out the gate

came down so hard, you see – the cops

went overboard on traffic stops

then not just scofflaws, many folks

were scared away, it was no joke

for what they did was alienate

they ran folks off, made some irate

they mixed up kids just having fun

with knuckleheads out doin' wrong

Guess they all look alike you see,

no difference was between them seen

. . .

and ran the black youth off the strip

though it was fine for white kids –hipster

beaches, blunts, and bacchanals

were all ok – now black kids gone

Mud Bashes were more welcomed than

the Hip-Hop dancin' on The Strand

Newcomers carved out their own beach

while young Detroiters had to leave

They made so many families flee

Things went too far, as one could see

that for a while it was all off-track

Some felt unwelcome, that's a fact

But now there is a balance back

restoring confidence, in fact

to welcome us, both White and Black

and all who want the island back

But some land's covered in cement

from yearly auto race events

and giant berms that block our way

too many months a year they stay

And rumor has it, there are those

who want our island for their own

to turn into their private isle

not now, but in a future while

I say to them, that if they should

old Holy Ghosts will rise for good

Those Spirits raise from the lagoon

To take your hands off our heirloom

For now new black folks dressed in white

do gather there in early light

assemble during crepuscule

to be immersed into the pool

They walk right down into the waves,

tradition, since we were enslaved

ancestors honored in the surf,

who used to walk on Belle Isle's turf

The rich will come to rue the day

they try to plunder Picnic Way

Regret the day they try to keep

Belle isle from us, to make us weep

No good will come from what they reap

The Spirits will rise from the deep

Rise from the creeks and streams and fjords

Revenge is mine, thus sayeth Lord

We call the Spirits of Detroit

To wrestle not with who'd exploit

for battle's not with them you see

but unseen principalities

Now that the island's more diverse

I summon all who hear this verse

to coalesce to keep Belle Isle

for *all* Detroiters all the while

No private island shall they make

exclusive playground for to take

restricted land just for their fun

no longer here for everyone

For there's still places to explore

and now, so much has been restored

The Fountain, Fish House, we can see

Their beauty's no hyperbole

Today we savor Belle Isle's peace

and watch the crossing ducks & geese

The Boat and Yacht Clubs renovate

(and they no longer segregate)

The island's quiet, right for bikes

And walking, running, evening hikes

A place for nationalities

The burkas, bubas, and saris

Each dawn Belle Island is reborn

the rowers set out in the morn

so quietly their vessels glide

the oars do pierce the morning tide

at Belle Isle's daybreak, full of dew

the early hour's mist in view

and flora, fauna, fanciful

the morning mist, so magical

Our island is a hallowed place

repository of the grace

bestowed, on Detroit's human race

Yes Belle Isle is a sacred place

Copyright – Marsha Music, 2016

5

JOLENE

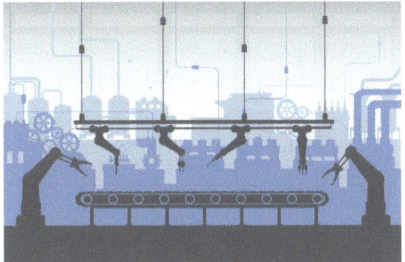

I once worked in a factory with a girl named Jolene. We were 17 and I had lied to get hired; we couldn't legally work in the plant for another year.

She was white, from somewhere around "Taylor-tucky", a name that mocked the southern roots of working class whites of the suburb of Taylor, Michigan. I lived in Detroit (still do). I was black, and I still am, as a matter of fact. Without the factory we'd never have met.

We were young and shapely then, which now, I'm not so much; I don't know about Jolene, I haven't seen her since those days in the '70's. She had just been hired at the plant, and – like they say it is, in prison – you depend on those who know the lay of the land, even if it's just a day more than you.

The factory, on a barren industrial stretch off of I-94, was a mechanized hell of extreme temperature, convoluted steel, and people at all levels with power, the wielding of which – for us – never did bode well. Women wore hairnets for "quality control", but mostly to prevent decapitation; the long-haired guys wore them too.

I wore old-fashioned braids weaved to my waist; the specter of hair and heads caught in rolling gears was so horrific, we all wore the ugly nets in willing resignation; just one more theft of our outside, normal lives.

Jolene and I circled each other with cat-like territoriality, two girls used to inhabiting the center of any attention. After a while, we relaxed in the knowledge that our appeal could be divvied up without threat – there were plenty of male eyes for the both of us. We became friends, revolving around each other like planets, the type of friendship that burns too hot to last.

Jolene was blond, the type of blond that's white in childhood, that leaves a fuzz of white on the arms and brows white as snow–what they call tow-headed. She had high cheekbones from a Nordic ancestor, or maybe some long ago blood of Native America that gave her face high hills and low valleys in all the right places.

She had a mole near her mouth and perfect teeth and she laughed all the time at everything when she wasn't mad about something. She was as beautiful as the mod girls in my teen magazines and proof that good looks were not exclusive to the rich and high class.

Ours was a work-hours friendship, walking our fast, hip-rolling walk down the cement runways of the packing lines, lithe and nubile. We flaunted our tiny waists and drum-tight thighs and switched past the high seniority ladies with tired feet and eyes, who had left their younger bodies back in some other lifetime.

We ate in the lunchroom, laughed and drove men crazy and pretended we didn't know. We held court with the tradesmen and machinists, flirted our way through the long, hard overtime days. Even so I was dead serious, in ceaseless examination of my surreal, hard surroundings – Alice fallen onto the wrong side of the looking glass, wanting to know just where and why I had landed.

I was forced into the blue-collar world by pregnancy at 16 and a hard-headed refusal to return to school – my post-sixties rebellion against the strictures of formal education, but also – though I'd never admit it – the humiliation of too-young motherhood. These were the days when there was still shame in such a thing.

The prospect of the factory met with the dismay of my businessman father and my mother (who at that point, had never worked a day in her life except a brief stint in his employ).

Mine had been the first black family on the block in Highland Park, a then- prosperous "suburb" in the middle of Detroit. My father was a record shop man amidst white bankers, salesmen, doctors–the solid middle class, in the days when that term didn't apply to blue collar folks, before proletarians had stock options and portfolios. As more of "us" moved into the neighborhood, my Talented Tenth peers were preparing and poised for success in the form of a piece of the professional American pie.

The bottom line is, working in a factory was not exactly what was expected of me.

Jolene was a young mother too. Though for me, young and unwed meant abandoning my destiny–for Jolene, from the poor and working class "down river" suburbs, it meant not escaping hers. If work in the plant was for me the fall from grace, for her it was the height of good fortune, key to a future other than trapped in a trailer home.

There were a handful of blacks in the plant, among them Miss

Loretta, a bashful, hard-working woman from Down South who called our job at the plant the "plant-ation"; Indiana, small and yellow, who could work faster than anyone but fell behind on purpose so they couldn't her wear out like the machines.

Fast Freddy dressed like a Technicolor pimp before he changed from his dancing clothes into his uniform each day; years later he had a 6-page spread in GQ magazine – largest in its history. There was brown-skinned Edna from Yazoo City, Mississippi, bright and funny, with sad eyes blacked from a husband's fists, before she finally got tired of it and he went to jail.

Big, slow, tie-tongued Bob, who never missed work; he was so soft-hearted that any woman so inclined could take all of his money, and we often did. Fine as wine Lynnette, who looked like a movie star and knew it; who dreamed to be a flight attendant and leave us behind in the factory (which eventually, she did).

In the plant, the Blacks were an island in a sea of suburban white and they kept their eyes on me, lest I prove to be too smart and fast for my own good or theirs, causing trouble with my brick sh***house body or rebelling against the ways that they'd learned to survive.

I was unaccustomed to the whites of the working class, and I eyed in amazement these folks at the plant too – Willadean with a Tennessee twang and black-dyed hair, who knew the most important things one could have were good work shoes and a good man.

There were white men born in towns Down South that had aimed dogs and hoses on brown girls like me, bikers in full regalia with chains on long wallets holding money and Zig-Zags, for long days of work and nights of play.

There were engineers and machinists, exacting and smug in the security of their skills, who more or less looked out for all of us—the machines and people—and we grudgingly looked up to them, even if some of them spent hunting season with the supervisors.

I managed a wary co-existence with all my new co-workers at first, then settled into the realization that they were all "just people". Eventually, I became their leader. But that's another story.

We wore skin tight, high-waist Levis, denim corsets that noosed our torsos into tight circles small enough for a man's hands to wrap around and touch fingers front to back. Even childbirth could not destroy our strong, young curves; motherhood only gave us more of what got us in trouble in the first place.

Our jeans were threadbare in all the right places that implied rubbing against all the wrong things. We were locked together in beauty and failure and rebellion. We never buttoned our uniforms; the white lab-coat hems flew behind us as we sashayed down cinder block halls. We raced past the women with wisdom and seniority to get to the source of real attention – the guys we looked right in the eyes as we smoked cigarettes on the loading docks, letting them think they were smarter than us and might have a chance, never letting on they were wrong on both counts.

Bras burned on TV and we didn't wear them, proud that no one could make us, and mostly, because they stood quite nicely on their own. A supervisor, Phil, had his eye on Jolene and I, and when we'd burst into his office to report a mishap on the line or stomped about some new imposition on our lives he'd sit up, unable to tear his eyes away from breast level, calling us "High Beams" as if he was being original. We'd roll our eyes and swivel back to our machines, letting him know that whatever he was thinking, it was out of the question.

When the line broke down or shut down early, we jumped in cars and hit the gravel road behind the plant, and flew to the bar where we'd we stay til last call. By closing time we'd be knee-deep in beer and Southern Comfort and 7-Up, or Jack Daniels with a Pepsi chaser (this was back in the days when I still ruined my liquor).

By closing time we'd be sloshed and stumbling, the bar full of eye-lined, hard-drinkin' women and wanna-be cowboys chained to assembly jobs and wives who read Harlequin Romances. Sometimes we'd sing, drunk and off-key:

"You picked a fine time to leave me Lucille…with four hungry children and a crop in the field….I've had some bad times been through some sad times, But this time the hurt it won't heal…You picked a fine time to leave me Lucille"

The jukebox was full of those Kenny Rodgers songs, and ballads of Elvis and Patsy Cline. Some barmaids could fight you like a man, and, by night's end, sawdust and sickness lined the bathroom floors.

I know I was watched by some God I didn't believe in at the time, on those nights after last call—a drive home to the Far East Side cold drunk on a coal black highway, hand over one eye to keep the center line of I-94 from blurring into two.

That I didn't die or kill, I now attribute to a force miraculous.

It was June – suddenly summer – and I'd been at the plant for six months. The weather turned glorious and I left it outside each day while I went in for the afternoon shift at three. Day after day I was missing the summer, getting off work at midnight, or two or three a.m. I should have been graduating, going to the prom, and here I was, punching a clock.

In an awful epiphany, it occurred to me that there was no more "summer vacation", like in school, year after year since kindergarten. In this new world of work you might get a week off, or two, but certainly not a whole summer. This revelation was a bad surprise, and hit me very hard.

Jolene and I were working in separate departments, and the summer heat combined with the inferno inside turned the plant into a sauna. Grease oozed from the gears of the conveyor belts and even up out of the bricks in the floor; both working and walking were a dangerous proposition. We toiled in a steam bath of production quotas, eight, ten, twelve hours a day.

Some vomited in the heat, some passed out, the supervisors handed out salt tablets. From the catwalk, you could see waves of heat quavering over our steaming heads; in the flat and flickering fluorescence light the sweating, moving limbs and machinery were a vision of a different kind of hell.

Angry conflicts spit into the air at the smallest provocation or supervisory order. There was talk of a walk-out but no one dared to face the wrath of the company and union both. Still, out in the parking lot on breaks and at lunchtime, parties sprang from trunks of cars and the backs of station wagons; 8-track tapes played Willie Nelson, Bowie, Marvin Gaye; the beer and weed hidden from the security guards – who got high among themselves.

In this cauldron of heat, rage and music, love affairs bubbled up among single and married alike; furtive grapplings behind storage rooms and rows of stacked wooden pallets, full-blown trysts during the midnight shift in motel rooms on the way home.

The next day was still hot – and you still went back to work.

One day, during a break-down on the line, I slipped away. Not far of course, for the line would start up and I'd better be there, or else. I hid behind boxes and machines to furiously read a page or two of Flaubert, Hegel, Hershey.

Not just me, for in the plant there were real scholars. Some discuss issues of the day like career diplomats from their designated spots in the lunchroom, while others study in silent, desperate reading, their brief and hungry moments of escape.

I looked for the best route to dodge the foreman and slipped through the back of the line, tipping careful on the oil-slick floors past the press where a lady had lost two fingers—one in one year and one the next, past the maintenance tool shed, over a skid of supplies, past bins of packing boxes, around the hi-lo shack. Finally, drenched in sweat, I reached my destination, the railcar dock.

Away from the suffocating heat in the plant, it was a fine June day of a hot and bright new summer. I blinked in the clean, clear sunlight, I could smell the hay used to pack equipment and the blue wildflowers and wheat that grew along the railroad tracks. The plant was built on old farmland and there was still a rural beauty to anything that had escaped the industrial maw.

The dock was a massive barn, high and open ended so train cars could be maneuvered in and out on tracks embedded in the floors. A car would be uncoupled, unloaded and emptied of raw materials, then days or weeks later, hitched up and rolled back down the tracks.

The train was a mammoth thing, wheels higher than the top of my head; a sleeping mastodon of black steel. Sometimes a car would be bright red or yellow depending on the cargo, or huge tankers filled with oil.

Young guys, restless and trapped in the plant on the hot summer days, would climb up the sides, twenty feet high, and smoke a joint on top of the car, unseen by nosy supervisors or worrisome chicks.

I listened closely; I was lucky today, all alone. I walked the length of the car and snatched off my hairnet, to feel the breeze blow cool through my braids.

A beam of sunshine from a vent in the roof made a square on the floor ahead of me, and I watched the motes of dust and grain float in a tube of light from the sky to the floor. I walked over and stood in the patch of sun, as if that square of floor-bound light held the last vestige of my life long-ago.

Suddenly, reality and self-pity swirled around me like snow in a globe—my ruined life, friends at proms and graduations, going to summer parties before running off to college, and here was I, a teenager with a child who refused to let parents or welfare help too much, now paying the price for my young lust and pride, defiant and rebellious, tying my fate to those who labored.

I looked into the light but the sun held no answers, I let the sweet June heat replace the steam-bath that I had left on the line. I saw myself, movie-like, from outside myself; a dark, lonely seraph in a column of defeat and light. In a few minutes, it was time to go back to the line.

Well, I thought, I'll stick it out a while longer, then decide what to do.

A dozen summers later I was still there.

I started out telling you about Jolene. It's been three decades since we met, and, actually, there's not much more to say; we stayed friends for a while before she was fired, or walked out of her own accord; her pretty smile didn't make up for her smart mouth after maybe too many beers or too much anger about a direct order she didn't want to follow.

I wonder if she started going with a man, the kind you couldn't be with and stay beautiful; you had to turn brittle and hard and ready to take a whippin'. I wonder if her face got that punched up look of too many schnapps and bar-fights, if her pretty teeth were gone; if she added many children to that first one, if she met up with cocaine.

Or, if her life turned different than the one she had; if it took an unexpected turn. She maybe ended up a lady with a cultured laugh and high cheekbones, with white-blond hair and pearls. In my memories she's still young; raw and beautiful as the hills.

I don't know what happened to her; after those first years of seniority I never saw her again. Even now, when I see a white-blond woman of means – or of no means – I think, sometimes, of Jolene. There's not much more to tell about her.

So maybe I told you about her so that I could tell you about me. For looking back, of course, my life was not near over, my factory days were clearly no defeat. It was just another row of pieces in the puzzle of my life, a twelve yearlong stop in my journey of years.

Maybe I just wanted you to know that once I was young with a waist so small a man's hands could fit all around, with thighs like congas and hip-length braids that blew in the breeze. Once upon a time I had another life.

I once worked in a factory with a girl named Jolene.

by Marsha Music

[This was originally posted on the BellesLettres forum of ThePurists.com, then, in 2002, published in the online magazine Counterpunch, thanks to editor Jeffrey St. Clair and music critic Dave Marsh.

"Jolene" was subsequently published in the hard-copy anthology Serpents In The Garden: Liaisons with Culture and Sex. It was one of my submissions for which I was awarded a Kresge Fellowship in the Literary Arts, in 2012.

It is a true tale about my days in a suburban Detroit factory, years ago, when I was young.]

ABOUT THE AUTHOR

MARSHA MUSIC

Marsha Music, daughter of legendary pre-Motown Detroit record producer Joe Von Battle, and Detroit West Side beauty Shirley Battle, was born in Detroit and grew up in Highland Park, Michigan - a city within the city of Detroit - during its lush days of industrial and civic prosperity. She has lived all of her life in these two cities. She is the eldest daughter of her father's second marriage, and in her youth, Marsha was a student activist, and later, a labor union president.

A Detroit cultural luminary, Ms. Music is a self-described "Detroitist" and writes about the city's music, past, current, and future on her eponymous blog. She is a noted presenter and storyteller, and has contributed to many literary anthologies, as well as oral histories, podcasts, voiceovers, television shows and films. In 2012, she was awarded a prestigious Kresge Literary Arts Fellowship, and in 2015 she received a Knight Arts award. She has presented her writings on many Detroit stages, including with the Detroit Symphony, and has received accolades for her one woman shows. She is also recognized as an exemplar of Detroit style.

Ms. Music is completing a long-awaited book about her father's record shops. Her essays and poems have been acclaimed for engaging readers in historical and contemporary narratives of Detroit, and her much noted works, *The Kidnapped Children of Detroit* and *Just Say Hi* are featured in this, her inaugural book.

www.ingramcontent.com/pod-product-compliance
Lightning Source LLC
LaVergne TN
LVHW010019070426
835507LV00001B/7